Spotlight on
Russia

Bobbie Kalman

🌳 Crabtree Publishing Company

www.crabtreebooks.com

Spotlight On My Country

Created by Bobbie Kalman

Dedicated by Emese Felvégi
For Kathy and Josh Matthew

Author and Editor-in-Chief
Bobbie Kalman

Research
Emese Felvégi

Editor
Kathy Middleton

Proofreader
Crystal Sikkens

Fact editor
Marcella Haanstra

Photo research
Bobbie Kalman
Emese Felvégi

Design
Bobbie Kalman
Katherine Berti

Print and production coordinator
Katherine Berti

Prepress technician
Katherine Berti

Illustrations
Katherine Berti: pages 4, 5 (map)

Photographs
BigStockPhoto: page 9 (nerpa)
Photos.com: pages 11 (bottom), 18 (bottom),
    19, 27 (bottom), 28 (bottom right)
Wikimedia Commons: Alekseev, Fedor
    Yakovlevich: page 15 (bottom left);
    Boris Kustodiyev: back cover, pages
    17 (inset), 27 (top); Maarten: page 23 (top)
Front cover and all other images by Shutterstock

Library and Archives Canada Cataloguing in Publication

Kalman, Bobbie, 1947-
    Spotlight on Russia / Bobbie Kalman.

(Spotlight on my country)
Includes index.
Issued also in an electronic format.
ISBN 978-0-7787-3460-4 (bound).--ISBN 978-0-7787-3486-4 (pbk.)

    1. Russia (Federation)--Juvenile literature. I. Title. II. Series:
Spotlight on my country

DK510.23.K34 2011   j947   C2010-904546-7

Library of Congress Cataloging-in-Publication Data

Kalman, Bobbie.
    Spotlight on Russia / Bobbie Kalman.
       p. cm. -- (Spotlight on my country)
    Includes index.
    ISBN 978-0-7787-3486-4 (pbk. : alk. paper) -- ISBN 978-0-7787-3460-4
(reinforced library binding : alk. paper) -- ISBN 978-1-4271-9539-5
(electronic PDF)
    1. Russia (Federation)--Juvenile literature. I. Title. II. Series.

DK510.23.K35 2011
947--dc22

2010027350

Crabtree Publishing Company

www.crabtreebooks.com   1-800-387-7650

Printed in the U.S.A./082010/BA20100709

Published in Canada
Crabtree Publishing
616 Welland Ave.
St. Catharines, Ontario
L2M 5V6

Published in the United States
Crabtree Publishing
PMB 59051
350 Fifth Avenue, 59th Floor
New York, New York 10118

Published in the United Kingdom
Crabtree Publishing
Maritime House
Basin Road North, Hove
BN41 1WR

Published in Australia
Crabtree Publishing
386 Mt. Alexander Rd.
Ascot Vale (Melbourne)
VIC 3032

Contents

Welcome to Russia!

Russia is the largest **country** in the world. A country is an area of land on which people live. It has **borders** that separate it from other countries. Russia shares its borders with several countries. China, Mongolia, Finland, and Norway are some of these. Find them on the map below. Russia is also bordered by two oceans. The Arctic Ocean is along its north coast, and the Pacific Ocean is on its east coast.

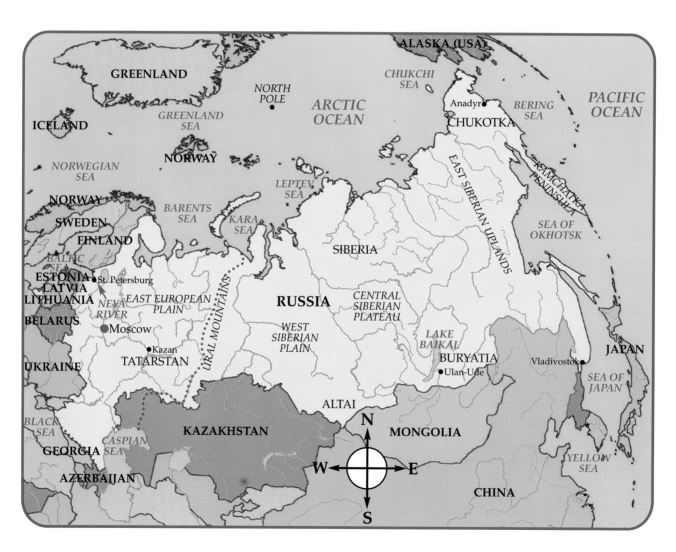

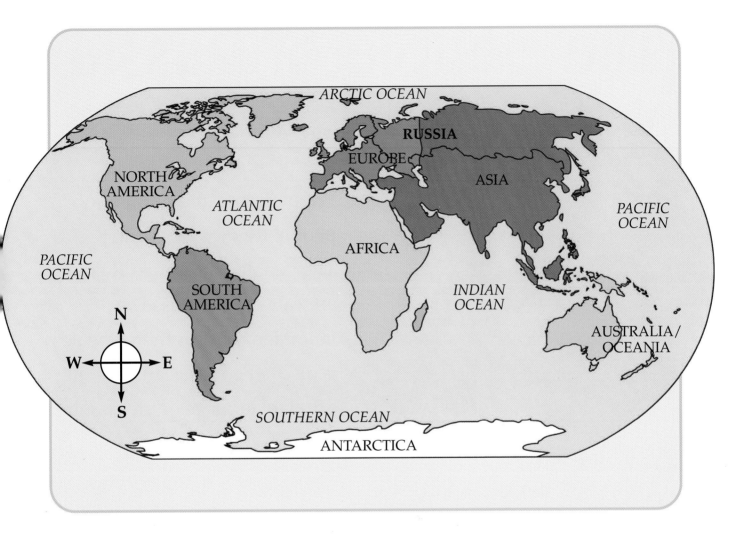

Where on Earth is Russia?

Russia is part of both Europe and Asia. The two **continents** are often called **Eurasia**. The other continents are North America, South America, Africa, Australia/Oceania, and Antarctica. The seven continents are shown on the world map above.

The people of Russia

The **population** of Russia is about 140 million people. Population is the number of people living in a country. The people who live in Russia are called Russians. The language most of them speak is also called Russian. It is the **official** language of the country.

This proud Russian grandfather is visiting Moscow's Red Square with his grandchildren. Red Square is one of the most-visited places in Russia. (See page 15.)

National groups

There are over 160 **national groups** living in Russia. National groups are people who share languages, beliefs, customs, and ways of life. More than three-quarters of the people in Russia are Russians. Other national groups are Tatars, Belarusians, Ukrainians, Buryats, and Bashkirs. The Inuit, Aleut, and Chukchi are groups that live in the most northern part of Russia.

calabash

This man is dressed in a uniform worn by Tatar soldiers long ago. He is holding a cup of water he poured from a container called a **calabash**.

This family lives in Buryatia in the southern part of Siberia. Buryatia is near Mongolia. There are close to a half-million Buryats living in this area.

This girl is a Chukchi. The Chukchi are **indigenous**, *or native, peoples who live near the Arctic Ocean in Chukotka and in other areas of Siberia. The Chukchi call themselves "Luoravetlan." This word means "true person." Inuit and Aleut people also live in the Arctic region of Russia.*

Russia's land

Russia is part of two continents—Europe and Asia. Its five main **regions**, or land areas, look very different. The European part of Russia has large, flat **plains** that are covered by grasses and forests. Russia's Ural Mountains separate Europe from Asia. Siberia is in the Asian part of Russia. It is made up of the West Siberian Plain, the Central Siberian **Plateau**, and the East Siberian **Uplands**. A plateau is a high, flat area, and uplands are high, hilly lands.

*These horses are **grazing**, or feeding on grasses, beside a mountain lake in Altai. Altai is in the southwest of Siberia and in the center of Asia. This area has grasslands, forests, deserts, and mountains.*

8

A bear on the hunt sits in front of a **volcano** on the Kamchatka **Peninsula**. There are over 300 volcanoes in Kamchatka, and 29 of them are **active**. Active volcanoes could erupt.

Winters on the Arctic **tundra** in Russia are long and cold. Tundra is frozen land. This Chukchi woman wears thick clothing made of animal furs to protect her from the freezing weather.

nerpa

Lake Baikal is the oldest **freshwater** lake in the world. Fresh water does not contain a lot of salt. Lake Baikal holds more water than any other lake—about one-fifth of Earth's fresh water. More than 1,100 plants and 1,500 to 1,800 types of animals live in its water, such as the Baikal seal. This seal, also known as a nerpa, is smaller than other seals. It is the only seal that does not live in salt water.

Plants and animals

There are three main **biomes**, or zones of plant life, in Russia. Each large zone also has its own types of animals. From north to south, these zones are the tundra, **taiga**, and **steppes**. Taiga are coniferous forests, and steppes are flat grasslands.

*Brown bears in Russia are among the largest bears. They can weigh as much as 790 lbs (360 kg). Brown bears are **omnivores**. They eat both plants and smaller animals. They live in the taiga.*

No trees grow on the tundra because it is very windy there, and the soil is frozen. These reindeer are searching for plants to eat under the snow.

The Siberian tiger

Siberian tigers, also called Amur tigers, live in the forests and river **valleys** of the Russian Far East. These tigers are the largest of all tigers. Very thick fur allows them to survive cold winters. Siberian tigers are endangered in the **wild**, or the natural places where they live. Most Siberian tigers live in **reserves**, or protected parks in Russia. Hundreds live in zoos.

*The Amur leopard lives in the mountainous areas of the taiga and in the forests of the Russian Far East. It is **critically endangered**, or in danger of dying out soon. There are not many of these leopards left.*

Country life

Fewer than one-quarter of Russia's people live in **villages**. A village is a small town in the countryside. Families who do live in the country often farm the land on which they live. They grow fruits and vegetables and raise animals for their meat, milk, eggs, or wool.

Farm children help their parents plant gardens and take care of vegetables. The girls in the top picture helped gather some apples. This girl is cutting some lettuce for lunch.

This country home is at the edge of a forest. Many vegetables are growing in the garden.

At the Ethnographic Museum near Lake Baikal, a group of people called "Old Believers" sing, dance, and cook traditional Russian foods for visitors. The Old Believers refused to follow the new rules made by the Orthodox Church in 1652 and had to escape from their homes so they could keep their faith. They built many new villages in Siberia. They were nicknamed "Semeiskie," which means "family."

Russia's two big cities

The Peterhof Palace, just outside Saint Petersburg, is known for its beautiful fountains and parks.

Most people in Russia live in cities. Some Russian cities are in Europe, and some are in Asia. Russia's two largest cities, Moscow and Saint Petersburg, are both in Europe. These old cities are filled with magnificent palaces built centuries ago.

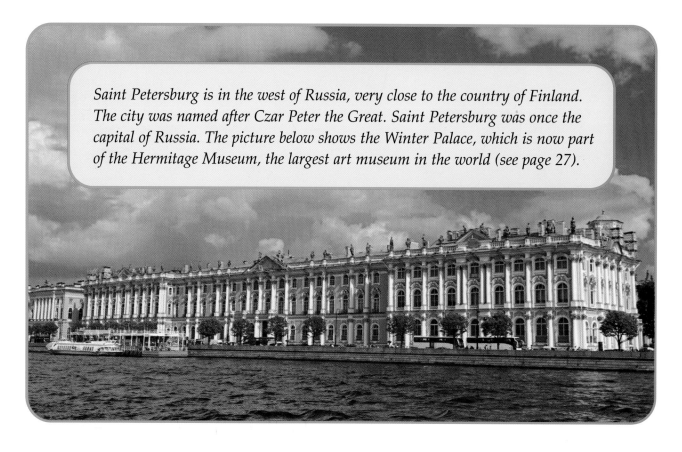

Saint Petersburg is in the west of Russia, very close to the country of Finland. The city was named after Czar Peter the Great. Saint Petersburg was once the capital of Russia. The picture below shows the Winter Palace, which is now part of the Hermitage Museum, the largest art museum in the world (see page 27).

Moscow Kremlin

State Historical Museum

GUM department store

Moscow is Russia's capital city. Red Square in Moscow was once the city's main marketplace. Today, the GUM department store has replaced the markets with beautiful, modern shops. The State Historical Museum is a museum of Russian history and art.

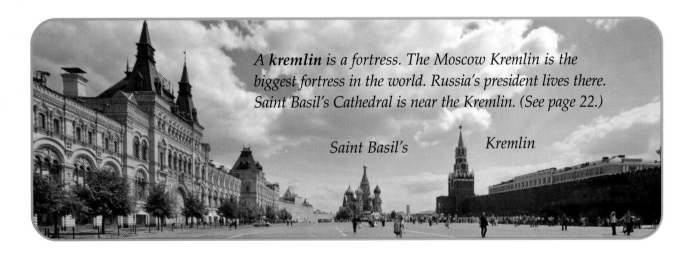

A **kremlin** is a fortress. The Moscow Kremlin is the biggest fortress in the world. Russia's president lives there. Saint Basil's Cathedral is near the Kremlin. (See page 22.)

Saint Basil's

Kremlin

This painting shows Red Square's marketplace long ago.

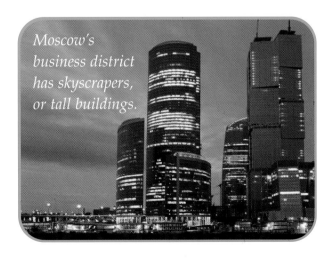

Moscow's business district has skyscrapers, or tall buildings.

Russia's early history

The Vikings were fierce warriors who took over much of Europe. They founded Kievan Rus. "Rus" later became "Russia."

Genghis Khan was a very famous Mongol leader. His grandson conquered Russia in 1237.

The Russians are descendants of people known as East Slavs. The East Slavs were farmers in Eastern Europe who settled throughout the lands that are now Russia. In 882, a group of Vikings invaded the Slavs and founded the kingdom of Kievan Rus. Years later, Mongols led by Batu Khan, the grandson of Genghis Khan, defeated the Vikings and ruled the land for 240 years.

Rule of the czars

In 1480, Russian Prince Ivan III, fought the Mongols and named himself **czar**, or emperor. During the rule of the czars, Russia gained control over lands that stretched from Eastern Europe to the Pacific Ocean. After 1613, all the czars came from the powerful Romanov family. The Romanovs ruled Russia for over 300 years.

The Romanovs

The Romanovs introduced Russia to modern ideas, arts, and **architecture**, or building design, that they copied from Western Europe. The czars lived royal lives, but they did not help the people of Russia. Most Russians were very poor and were not able to own any land. Nicholas II was Russia's last czar. He gave up power in 1917. He and his family were **executed**, or killed, in 1918.

Czar Nicholas II was born in 1868 and was crowned czar in 1894. He ruled until 1917, when he was forced to give up his power.

The Romanovs lived in spectacular palaces, such as the Catherine Palace, while most Russians led very poor lives.

The Soviet Union

By the 1900s, the Russian people no longer wanted to live like slaves under the czars. In 1917, a **communist** leader named Vladimir Ilyich Lenin took control. He formed the Soviet Union, or the Union of Soviet Socialist Republics (U.S.S.R.) in 1922. Life was still very difficult for most Russians, however. They could not speak freely, travel to other countries, or practice their religions.

*Lenin led Russia into a **revolution**, or war against the government, which lasted from 1917 to 1921. This painting shows the Russian people attacking the Winter Palace of the czars.*

What is communism?
In a communist country, the government makes most of the decisions for the people. It decides which crops are grown on farms, which products are made in factories, and where people will live. People cannot choose their leaders or decide how their country should be run. People do not feel free, and they do not feel safe. The red star is the symbol of communism. It represents the five fingers of the workers.

Lenin's communist government formed the U.S.S.R. Russia and 14 neighboring countries became part of the U.S.S.R. Everyone in these countries was forced to follow the rules of the government in Moscow, but the worst was yet to come! Stalin became the next leader.

Stalin, the monster

Joseph Stalin become the leader of the Soviet Union in the years following Lenin's death in 1924. Stalin terrorized and executed millions of people, including many of his friends. He put millions more into labor camps, or prisons. He forced farmers to give up their crops to sell outside Russia, causing them to starve to death. The Russian people suffered horribly under his rule, until he died in 1953.

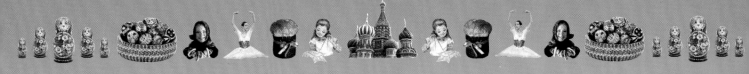

Russia today

*The flag of Russia is white, blue, and red. A flag that has three colors is called a **tricolor**.*

In 1991, the U.S.S.R. split into Russia and 14 other countries. Russia is no longer communist. It is a **democracy**. A democracy is a country in which people **elect**, or vote for, their own leaders. Within Russia are 21 **republics** and a number of other areas. These republics and other areas are allowed certain freedoms, such as speaking their own languages and practicing their cultures, but they are all still governed by Russia.

*Russia's government members are called **deputies**. The Russian parliament meets in the Duma building.*

Qol-Sarif
Mosque

The Republic of Tatarstan is part of Russia. Its capital city is Kazan. Tatar and Russian are the languages spoken in this republic. This picture shows the Kazan Kremlin. This large fortress contains an Islamic mosque. Most Tatars are Muslims who follow the religion of Islam.

The Republic of Altai has thousands of rivers, more than 7,000 lakes, and high mountains. Some Altai raise sheep and goats and move from place to place, but most live in one place.

Buryatia is a republic that is north of Mongolia. Buryats speak Buryat, which is a form of Mongol and Russian. These Buryats are doing a folk dance in colorful traditional costumes.

Religion in Russia

Some Russians follow religions such as Islam, Judaism, or Buddhism, but most people belong to the Russian Orthodox Church. Saint Basil's Cathedral, shown left, is Russia's most famous Orthodox church. It has the shape of a fire's flames. There are no other cathedrals like this in Russia. Saint Basil's is located in Moscow's Red Square (see page 15).

*These people are celebrating the finding of an old religious **icon**, or sacred artwork, which shows Mary and Jesus. In towns and villages, often the whole community takes part in religious processions.*

(below) The Temple of All Religions in Kazan combines a mosque, church, pagoda, synagogue, and twelve other religious houses into one building. Religious services are not held here. This building shows that people of all religions have similar beliefs.

Many Buryats are Buddhists who follow Tibetan Buddhism.

This picture shows a Buddhist monastery in Buryatia. It is called "Temple of the Pure Land."

Russia's culture

Russian **culture** is a blend of European and Asian cultures. Culture is the beliefs, customs, and ways of life that are shared by a group of people. People celebrate their cultures in stories, sports, dance, music, clothing, food, and holidays. The Russian calendar is filled with holidays and other celebrations!

folk dancer

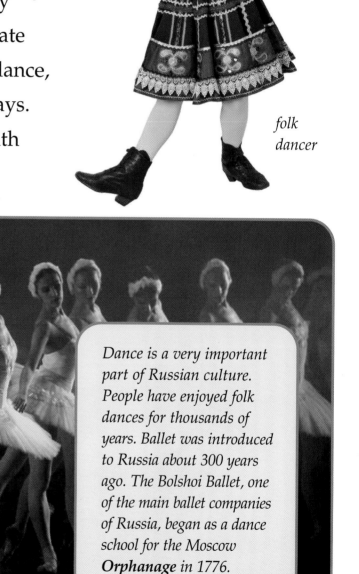

*Dance is a very important part of Russian culture. People have enjoyed folk dances for thousands of years. Ballet was introduced to Russia about 300 years ago. The Bolshoi Ballet, one of the main ballet companies of Russia, began as a dance school for the Moscow **Orphanage** in 1776.*

In spring, most of Russia's people celebrate Easter. Painted eggs are part of their Easter celebrations. Eggs stand for new life. Spring is the time when nature comes back to life.

Russia's national groups have their own cultures. This Chukchi man is doing a traditional drumming dance. He is part of the Chukchi-Eskimo Ergyron dance and song group, created in 1968 in Chukotka.

These boys are playing hockey, a popular sport in Russia. Many Russian players are stars in the National Hockey League, which has skilled players from about 20 different countries.

Art in Russia

Russia's rich tradition of art includes religious paintings, modern art, and film. Russian **artisans**, or craftspeople, have also made many kinds of folk art, including clothing, toys, and items for the home.

Fabergé eggs are named after Peter Carl Fabergé, the Russian jeweler who made them. Each egg has a surpise hidden inside.

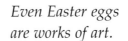

Even Easter eggs are works of art.

*A matryoshka doll is a nesting doll that has smaller- and smaller-sized dolls hidden inside. The dolls are sometimes called **babushka** dolls. Babushka means grandmother in Russian.*

*This beautifully painted **samovar** was used to heat water for tea.*

Russian artists

Russia has many famous artists. Boris Kustodiev painted pictures showing how people lived. Kustodiev painted this picture in 1918. It is called "The Merchant's Wife at Tea" and shows a woman enjoying the popular Russian tradition of tea drinking. She made the tea in a samovar.

The Hermitage

The Hermitage Museum in Saint Petersburg houses one of the biggest art collections in the world (see page 14). More than three million works of art are in this museum. Among them are paintings by famous European artists, such as Auguste Renoir, who painted this picture, called "Boy With a Whip."

The tastes of Russia

Food is an important part of a country's culture. Traditional Russian meals always start with a soup, followed by meats and vegetables. Fish and **caviar**, or fish eggs, are popular foods. Cakes or pancakes are served for dessert.

These fish sandwiches are made with smoked salmon and herring. These fish are eaten often by Russians.

Russians bake many kinds of cakes. This huge cake is a work of art!

Borscht is a favorite soup in Russia. It is made with beets.

These girls have made a pile of pancakes for Pancake Week.

Most pancakes have sweet fillings, but these pancakes are made with caviar.

*These girls each have a long line of **cracknel**, or round biscuits, tied around their necks. People wear cracknel "necklaces" like these during Pancake Week to celebrate the end of winter.*

Russia's children

Children are the center of the Russian family. Parents try to give them every chance to have good lives. Getting a good education is at the top of that list. Children start school at the age of seven, but many also go to preschool. Those with a talent in a particular area are often sent to special schools, such as ballet school or language school.

Children work on computers, just as you do. These girls are doing some research for a science report.

This boy is visiting the Sochi Arboretum, a place where many kinds of trees and other plants grow, including pine, oak, and palm. These plants are bamboo. Bamboo is a woody grass.

These boys are fishing with their grandfather. They will eat the fish they catch for dinner.

This girl lives in the country. She is helping her family take care of some baby chicks.

31

Glossary

Note: Some boldfaced words are defined where they appear in the book.

biome A large natural area that contains certain types of plants and animals

continent One of Earth's seven large areas of land

critically endangered Describing an animal species that is close to dying out

culture The beliefs, customs, and ways of life of a group of people

democracy A system of government in which people vote for their leaders

Eurasia Referring to the continents Europe and Asia as one large continent

fresh water Water that does not contain a lot of salt

indigenous Describing people who are the first to live in an area

official Describing something that is approved by a government

omnivore An animal that eats both plants and other animals

orphanage A place where children who have no parents live

peninsula A piece of land that has water almost all the way around it

population The total number of people living in a certain area

republic A state in which people have the freedom to practice non-Russian cultures

steppe A flat grassland with a few trees

taiga A northern evergreen forest, which starts where a tundra ends

tundra A treeless area in an Arctic region that has permanently frozen soil

valley A flat area below mountains

village A small town in the country that does not have many buildings or people

volcano An opening in Earth's crust, where hot liquid rock flows out

Index